Khufu's Pyramid
And The
Sphinx

FACES
AND
PLACES

EGYPT

BY PATRICK RYAN

THE CHILD'S WORLD®, INC.

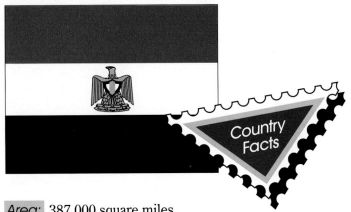

Country
Facts

Area: 387,000 square miles.
That is about the size of Texas and California put together.

Population: About 63 million people.

Capital City: Cairo.

Other Important Cities: Alexandria, Giza, Aswan, Luxor.

Money: The Egyptian pound.

National Language: Arabic.

National Songs: "Belady, Belady," or "My Homeland, My Homeland."

National Flag: Red, white and black with a golden eagle in the middle. The red stands for Egypt's deserts. The black stands for the rich farmlands near the Nile.

Long Name: Arab Republic of Egypt. People just say "Egypt" for short.

Heads of Government: President Mohammed Hosni Mubarak and Prime Minister Kamal Ahmed al–Ganzouri.

Text copyright © 1999 by The Child's World®, Inc.
All rights reserved. No part of this book may be reproduced or utilized in any form or by any means without written permission from the publisher.
Printed in the United States of America.

Library of Congress Cataloging-in-Publication Data
Ryan, Pat (Patrick M.)
Egypt / by Patrick M. Ryan.
Series: "Faces and Places".
p. cm.
Includes index.
Summary: An introduction to the geography, history, culture, and people of Egypt.
ISBN 1-56766-514-4 (library reinforced : alk. paper)

1. Egypt — Juvenile literature.
[1. Egypt.] I. Title.

DT49.R97 1998
932 — dc21

97-46183
CIP
AC

GRAPHIC DESIGN
Robert A. Honey, Seattle

PHOTO RESEARCH
James R. Rothaus / James R. Rothaus & Associates

ELECTRONIC PRE–PRESS PRODUCTION
Robert E. Bonaker / Graphic Design & Consulting Co.

PHOTOGRAPHY
Cover photo: Egyptian Boy With Donkey by Owen Franken/Corbis

Table of Contents

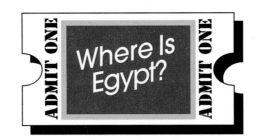

Where Is Egypt?

If you were an astronaut circling Earth, you would see huge land areas surrounded by water. These land areas are called **continents**. One of Earth's continents is Africa. It is made up of many different countries. One large country on the continent of Africa is Egypt.

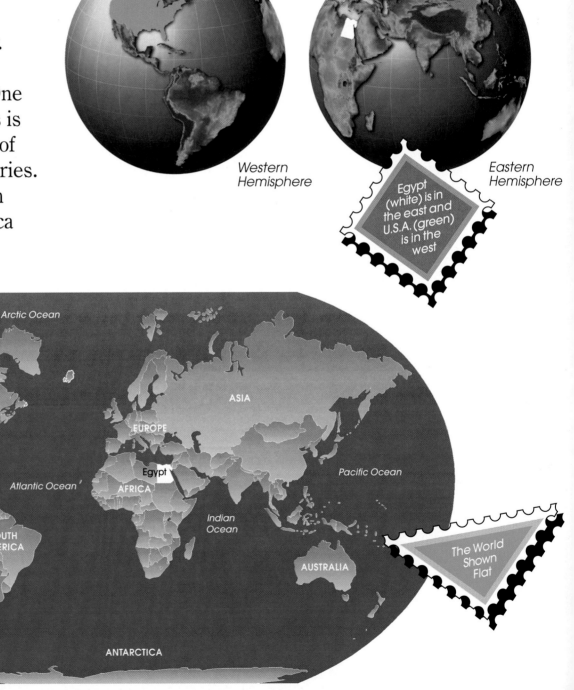

Western Hemisphere

Eastern Hemisphere

Egypt (white) is in the east and U.S.A. (green) is in the west

Arctic Ocean

NORTH AMERICA

United States of America

Atlantic Ocean

Pacific Ocean

SOUTH AMERICA

EUROPE

ASIA

Egypt

AFRICA

Indian Ocean

Pacific Ocean

AUSTRALIA

ANTARCTICA

The World Shown Flat

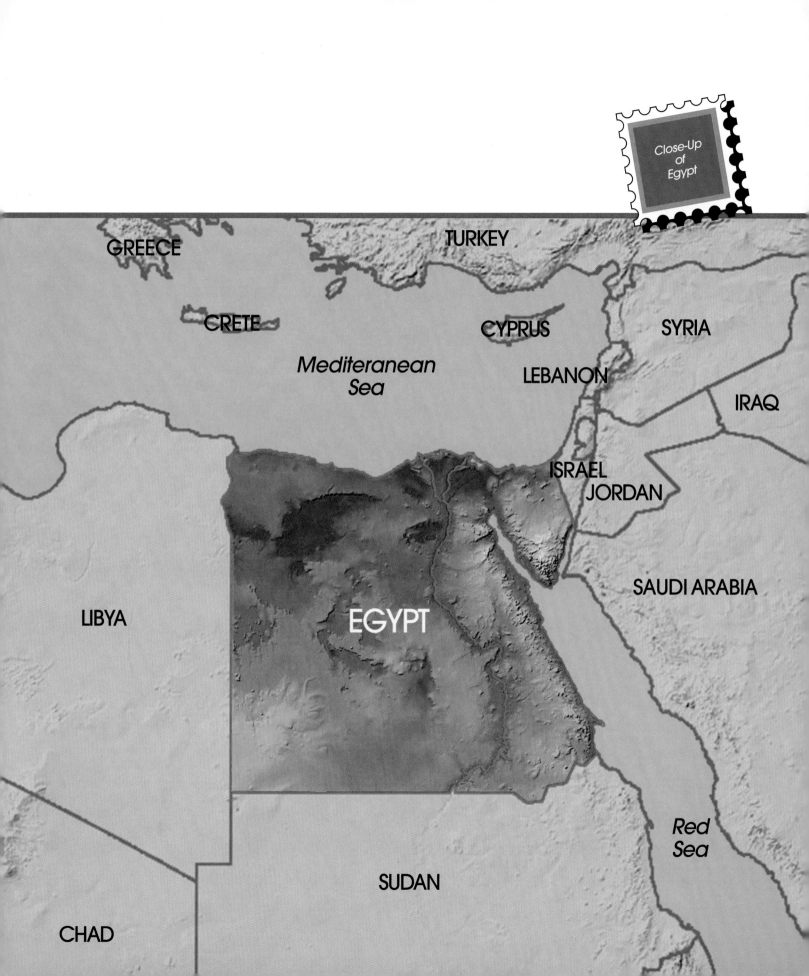

The Nile
Near
Elephantine
Island

Bahariya
Oasis●

+ Gebel
Baraka

WESTERN
DESERT

Nile River

N

Elephantine Island●

Jonathan Blair/Corbis

The Land

Desert Oasis At Bahariya

Yann Arthus-Bertrand/Corbis

Egypt is very hot and dry. Most of the land is covered with sandy deserts. In fact, Egypt's *Western Desert* makes up more than half of the whole country!

Steve Kaufman/Corbis

Desert Cliffs Near Gebel (Mount) Baraka

Yann Arthus-Bertrand/Corbis

Sand Dunes In The Western Desert

Egypt also has winding rivers. The Nile River is the most important river in Egypt. Many people and animals depend on its waters for drinking and cleaning. The Nile is also important because it brings water for Egypt's crops. The Nile is very different from most of the world's rivers. It flows north instead of south.

Desert Camels Of The Sinai

Jeffrey L. Rotman/Corbis

Most of Egypt's plants and trees like the hot, dry weather. Sycamore, tamarisk, and acacia trees all do well in that climate. But near the Nile, different kinds of plants are found. Cypress, eucalyptus and fruit trees all grow in the rich soil. Colorful flowers such as lotus and jasmine live along the water's edge.

Bottlenose Dolphin In The Red Sea

Jeffrey L. Rotman/Corbis

Nile Crocodiles

Wolfgang Kaehler/©Corbis

Many animals make Egypt their home. The most famous of these creatures is the camel. Camels can go for long periods of time without drinking water. Egypt also has many reptiles. Crocodiles and poisonous snakes often live near the Nile.

Giza
SINAI
RED
SEA
Nile River

Palm Trees
On Water's Edge
Near Giza

The
Great Pyramids
Of Giza

Cairo
Giza

Temple Of
Queen
Hatshepsut

Abu Simbel

Temple Of Ramses II At Abu Simbel

Richard T. Nowitz/Corbis

People have been living in Egypt for a very long time. Thousands of years ago, kings and queens called **pharaohs** ruled the land. The pharaohs lived in fancy palaces and were very wealthy. When a pharaoh died, he or she was buried in a giant tomb. The tomb was hidden inside a huge stone building called a **pyramid**. Some pyramids were as high as a 10–story building!

Temple Of Queen Hatshepsut

Mask Of Tutankhamun In The Cairo Museum

Papilio/Corbis

Roger Wood/©Corbis

Modern Skyscrapers Fill Alexandria

Yann Arthus-Bertrand/Corbis

Over the years, the pharaohs lost their power. Other countries began to rule Egypt. After many wars and many years of fighting, the people of Egypt began to rule their own country. Today, Egypt is at peace with its neighbors. It has a president and a prime minister instead of a pharaoh. The president and the prime minister work together with the government to make laws that keep Egypt safe.

Ocean Freighters In Suez Canal

Radio/TV Building In The Capital City Of Cairo

Dean Conger/Corbis

Dave Bartruff/Corbis

Cruise Ship At Today's City Of Aswan

Girl Selling Shells At Lake Moeris

Cairo
Lake Moeris
Nile River

Richard T. Nowitz/Corbis

Muslims Gathered For Prayer In Cairo

Robert Holmes/Corbis

Egypt is a land of old ways and new ways. Some Egyptians live in simple homes and raise animals. Others live in big cities with fast cars and busy shops.

A Packed Ferry Crosses The Nile

Ecoscene/Corbis

Religion is a very important part of the Egyptian way of life. Most Egyptians are *Muslims*. They pray five times a day. During prayer time, Muslims stop whatever they are doing. They kneel down and pray quietly to themselves.

City Dwellers On Shady Cairo Street

Jack Fields/Corbis

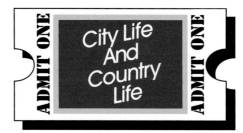

Sinai Bedouin Children In Front Of Tent

Jeffrey L. Rotman/Corbis

About half of all Egyptians live in cities. In fact, the Egyptian city of Cairo is one of the largest cities in the world! Many of the buildings in Egypt's cities are old. And like other cities of the world, there are problems with pollution. But the government of Egypt is working to make Cairo and other big cities better places to live.

Egypt's country people are called *fellahin* (feh–luh–HEEN). They often live in brick homes with metal roofs. The *Bedouins* (BEH–doh–winz) are country people, too. But they are **nomads**, or wanderers. Instead of houses, Bedouins live in tents. They travel from place to place with their herds of sheep, goats, and camels.

Painted House In The Nile Delta Area

Yann Arthus-Bertrand/Corbis

Country Homes In Qurna

© Corbis

Yann Arthus-Bertrand/Corbis

Alexandria ● ■ Nile Delta
Cairo ★ SINAI

Qurna ●

City Buildings In
Alexandria

Bedouin
Classroom
In The
Sinai

Jeffrey L. Rotman/Corbis

Teacher And Class In Port Said

Christine Osborne/Corbis

In many ways, school in Egypt is much like school in the United States. Children learn science, math, social studies, and music just as you do. But on Fridays, Egyptian schools are closed. That is because Fridays are special days of rest for many Egyptian families.

Pottery Studio In Harraniyah Art School

Egypt's official language is Arabic. It is a very old language that has been spoken for thousands of years. Many people also speak English.

Corbis-Bettmann

Finding The Rosetta Stone In 1799...

Made Reading Ramses II's Name In Hieroglyphics Possible

Richard T. Nowitz/Corbis

Richard T Nowitz/Corbis

Work

Egyptians are good at farming, but the weather is very hot and dry for growing crops. To help their crops grow better, the farmers use pipes to bring water to their fields. This is called **irrigation**. With the help of irrigation, Egyptian farmers raise such crops as sugarcane, cotton, dates, and olives.

Robert Holmes/Corbis

Oil is another product of the desert. Oil is very important and is needed for many different things. Most of the oil that comes out of Egypt is sent to special factories that turn it into gas. Then it is sent all over the world to be used by millions of people.

Donkey Irrigates Field Near Ancient Memphis

Boy With His Goatherd In Cairo

Jonathan Blair/Corbis

Alfalfa Harvest In Deir Abu Magar

Dave Bartruff/Corbis

Damietta
Memphis · ★ Cairo

Deir Abu Magar ·

Nile River

Fishing
Boats
On The
Nile At
Damietta

Making Kebabs In Matruh

Matruh

★Cairo

Luxor

Eye Ubiquitous/Corbis

Food

Cairo Lemonade Seller

Sean Sexton Collection/Corbis

Dave Bartruff/Corbis

Baking Bread In Cairo

Egyptian meals are delicious. Most dishes are made with lamb and vegetables. Another popular meal is *ful*, a dish made with beans and tomatoes. Many Egyptians eat ful every day—even for breakfast. Egyptians also like bread. But Egyptian bread is different. It is flat instead of high and springy. It is sometimes made with corn flour, eggplant, and yogurt.

Fruit Stand In Luxor

Richard T. Nowitz/Corbis

Egyptians love to have fun. They often play sports such as tennis, golf, and basketball. They also like to race horses and go sailing on the Nile. But the most popular pastime is soccer. In Egypt, you can find people playing soccer in the streets, in the schoolyards, and even in the countryside. Soccer is everywhere!

Boys Playing Soccer At Pyramid In Giza

Jack Fields/Corbis

Bathing Beach Near Alexandria

Robert Holmes/Corbis

The Purcell Team/Corbis

Alexandria
Giza
Nile River
Aswan

Sailboats
On Nile
Near
Aswan

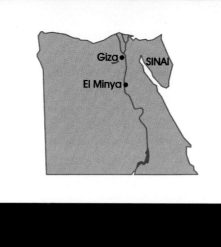

Sinai Bedouins Sing
For Ramadan

Holidays

Many of Egypt's holidays are special days in the Muslim religion. *Ramadan* is a holiday that is over a month long. During Ramadan, Muslims do not eat or drink during the day. Then, when the sun goes down, everyone in the house eats a huge meal. Ramadan is a little like Thanksgiving day 40 times in a row.

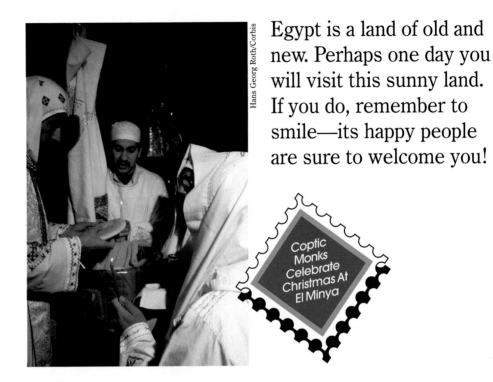

Hans Georg Roth/Corbis

Egypt is a land of old and new. Perhaps one day you will visit this sunny land. If you do, remember to smile—its happy people are sure to welcome you!

Coptic Monks Celebrate Christmas At El Minya

Dean Conger/Corbis

Guides Offer Camel Rides At Giza

An **oasis** is an area in the desert that has water. Water bubbles up from deep underground to make the oasis green with grasses and palm trees. Egypt has several oases. Long ago, wanderers would stop and rest with their camels at these cool "rest stops."

Long ago, Egyptians used a written language called **hieroglyphics** (hy–roh–GLI–fiks). By writing pictures in a certain order, Egyptians could leave messages or tell stories about anything they wanted to.

Each year, thousands of people come to see the Great Sphinx in Egypt's desert. The Sphinx is a huge statue that has the head of a person and the body of a lion. It is thought to be a monument to a great pharaoh of long ago. The Great Sphinx is about 5,000 years old.

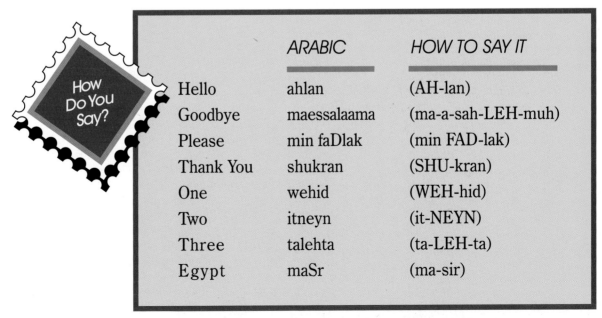

	ARABIC	HOW TO SAY IT
Hello	ahlan	(AH-lan)
Goodbye	maessalaama	(ma-a-sah-LEH-muh)
Please	min faDlak	(min FAD-lak)
Thank You	shukran	(SHU-kran)
One	wehid	(WEH-hid)
Two	itneyn	(it-NEYN)
Three	talehta	(ta-LEH-ta)
Egypt	maSr	(ma-sir)

Glossary

continents (KON–tih–nents)
The largest land areas on Earth are called continents. Egypt is on the continent of Africa.

hieroglyphics (hy–roh–GLI–fiks)
Long ago, Egyptians used a kind of writing called hieroglyphics. It used shapes and pictures instead of words.

irrigation (eer–ih–GAY–shun)
Irrigation uses pipes and pumps to bring water to fields. Many Egyptian farmers must use irrigation or their crops will die.

nomads (NOH–madz)
Nomads are people who travel from place to place instead of settling down. Nomads in Egypt travel with their herds of goats and sheep.

oasis (oh–AY–sis)
An oasis is an area in the desert that has water. An oasis is often green with grass and trees.

pharaohs (FAIR–ohz)
Long ago, the rulers of Egypt were called pharaohs. Pharaohs lived in fancy palaces and were very wealthy.

pyramids (PEER–uh–midz)
Pyramids are huge triangle–shaped buildings that were built long ago. The pyramids were used as tombs for the pharaohs.

Index